Let's Go To Mars!

Written by Janice Marriott

Illustrated by Mark Ruffle

Contents

Collins

Mars – it's different!

 Join us on our popular space flight to the red planet.

 See the largest **volcano** in the **solar system**. It's three times higher than Earth's highest mountain, Mount Everest.

 Go where the sky is red instead of blue.

 Join the hunt for life on Mars.

Mars – the facts

Mars is the fourth planet from the Sun. Earth is the third.

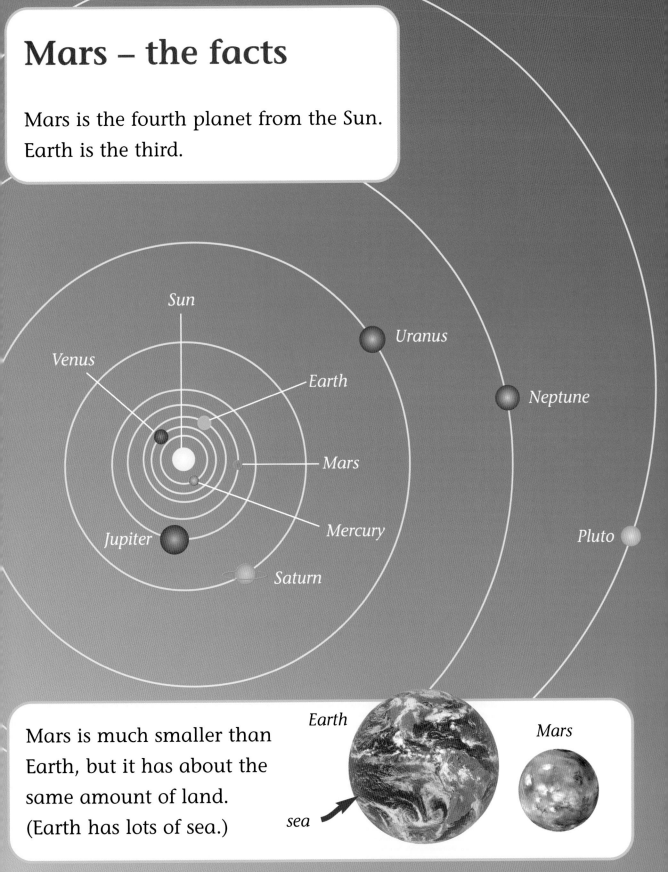

Sun

Uranus

Venus

Earth

Neptune

Mars

Jupiter

Mercury

Pluto

Saturn

Mars is much smaller than Earth, but it has about the same amount of land. (Earth has lots of sea.)

Earth

Mars

sea

What's the difference?

Mars is different from Earth, but not too different. It's not a ball of fire, like the Sun.

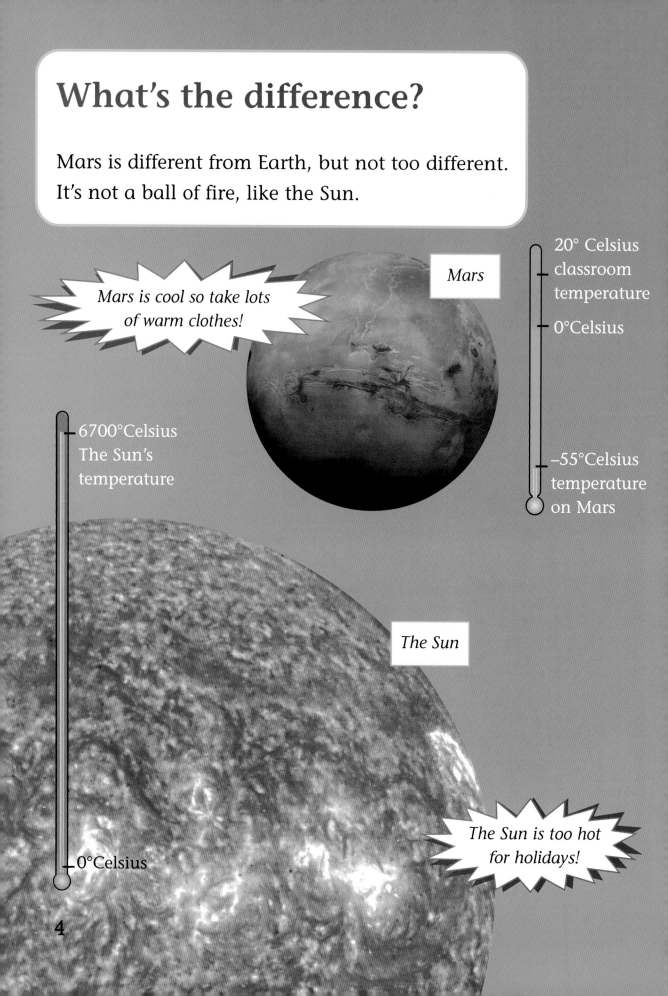

Mars is cool so take lots of warm clothes!

Mars

20° Celsius classroom temperature

0°Celsius

−55°Celsius temperature on Mars

6700°Celsius The Sun's temperature

The Sun

0°Celsius

The Sun is too hot for holidays!

Like Earth, Mars has air, water, ice and rock.

Unlike Mars, most of the Earth's surface is water.

Mars' surface is hard and dry.

Try sand-sailing on Mars' red sand.

Earth has living things in the oceans, on land and in the air. No living thing has been found anywhere on Mars ... yet.

Earth

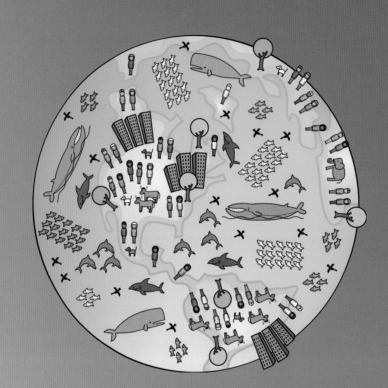

Mars

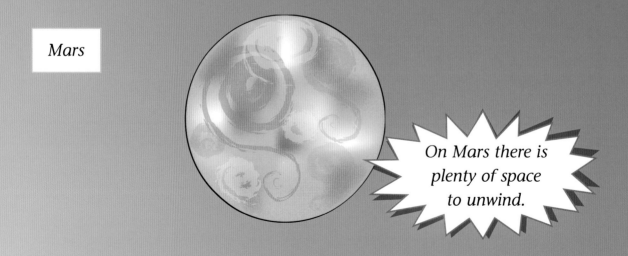

On Mars there is plenty of space to unwind.

Mars has **polar ice caps**, like Earth.

Mars can get colder than the South Pole – the coldest place on Earth.

Come to Mars!
It's so cool, it's freezing.

0°Celsius

−48°Celsius: South Pole average temperature
−55°Celsius: temperature on Mars

Mars has strong winds and lots of sand.
There's so much wind and sand that giant sand dunes
travel across the planet like huge, moving hills.

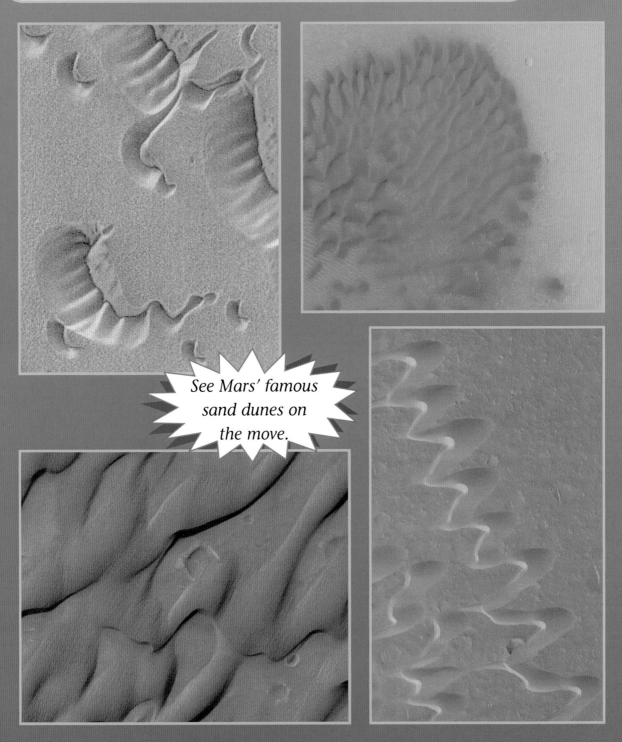

See Mars' famous sand dunes on the move.

You can breathe the air on Earth.
You can't breathe the air on Mars.
It would be like breathing car fumes all the time.

Your journey to Mars

We offer two different ways to get there:
Non-stop from Earth …

or …

with a stopover on the Moon.

We'll photograph you standing beside
the first footprint on the Moon.

It could be YOUR!

Your spaceship

You'll travel in comfort and safety in the latest spaceship. It has an extra-light, extra-strong skin that can repair itself if **space junk** hits it.

We give you a choice of travelling on the five-month-long flight, or the Mars Express that will take you to Mars in just three months.

In-flight entertainment

Enjoy the in-flight entertainment, including:

- floating toothpaste,
- breakfast in a bottle,
- weightless football.

Our on-board designer **spacesuit** bends with you, letting you have weightless fun.

Wear our outdoor spacesuit on space walks.

Your hard outdoor jacket is hanging on the wall. When you want to go out for a walk, you just rise up into it, buckle up and off you go.

I'm floating in space.

Transfers

Your spaceship will **orbit** Mars while we transfer you to the landing vehicle.

Parachutes and rockets will slow the spaceship from 16,000 kilometres per hour to 40 kilometres per hour, ready for landing.

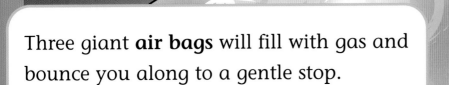

Three giant **air bags** will fill with gas and bounce you along to a gentle stop.

The air bags will separate, like the petals of a flower.

Then you can drive off and explore the planet in your own Mars Rover.

Mars Time

Time flies when you're on holiday – but not on Mars!

A Martian day is 37 minutes longer than on Earth so your bedtime will be later. A Martian year is twice as long as an Earth year.

Earth	Mars
1 year = 365 days	1 year = 730 days
1 day = 24 hours	1 day = 24 hours and 37 minutes

What to wear

Be cool on Mars!

Our spacesuits come complete with:

A **helmet** with **headphones** and **microphones** so you can talk to your family on Earth

A stretchy undersuit with zip front and water-cooling tubes to keep you at the right temperature

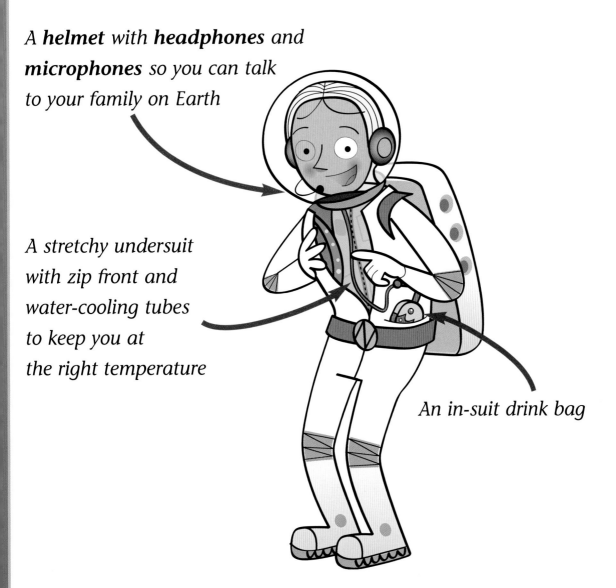

An in-suit drink bag

(Please note: If you want to phone home, you'll have to wait almost 25 minutes for the person back on Earth to hear you.)

What can you do on Mars?

Check out these fun holiday activities.

Build sand castles.

Enter the dune buggy races.

Set a land speed record
in a sand yacht.

Be blown about in
gigantic sandstorms.

Hunt for signs of water.

Watch red sunsets in a pink sky. The Sun will look half as big as it does from Earth.

Look for signs of life.

Have your photo taken under our sign.

Come with us – it's the best holiday in the solar system.

It's a lot better than Saturn, Jupiter and Pluto.

Come to Mars!

How much?
It's a bargain!

A child's fare is only 1,000 times more than a flight from London to Sydney, Australia.

That's cheap for an out-of-this-world experience.

All trips are return trips.

Make your booking today and start saving!

Mars Express

Picture Glossary

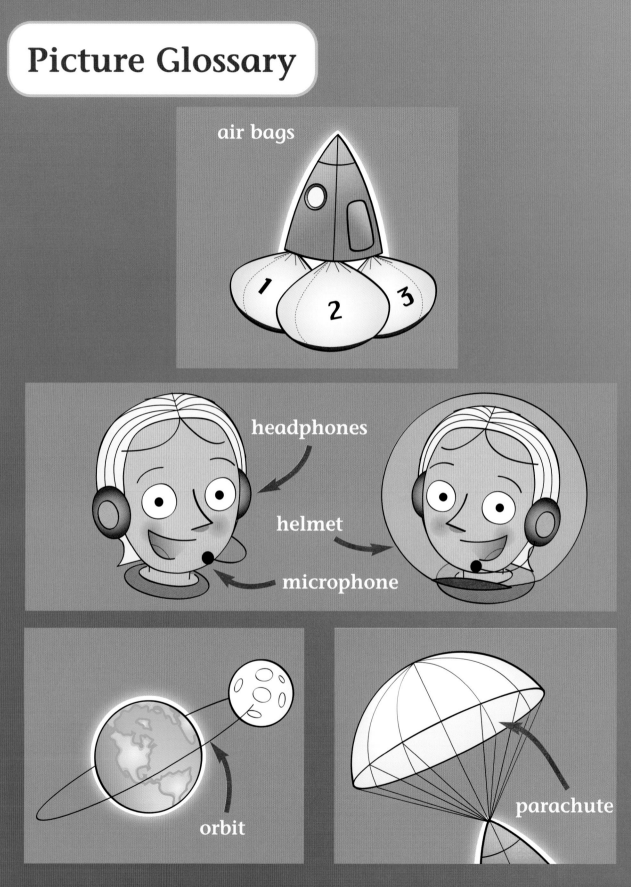

air bags

headphones

helmet

microphone

orbit

parachute

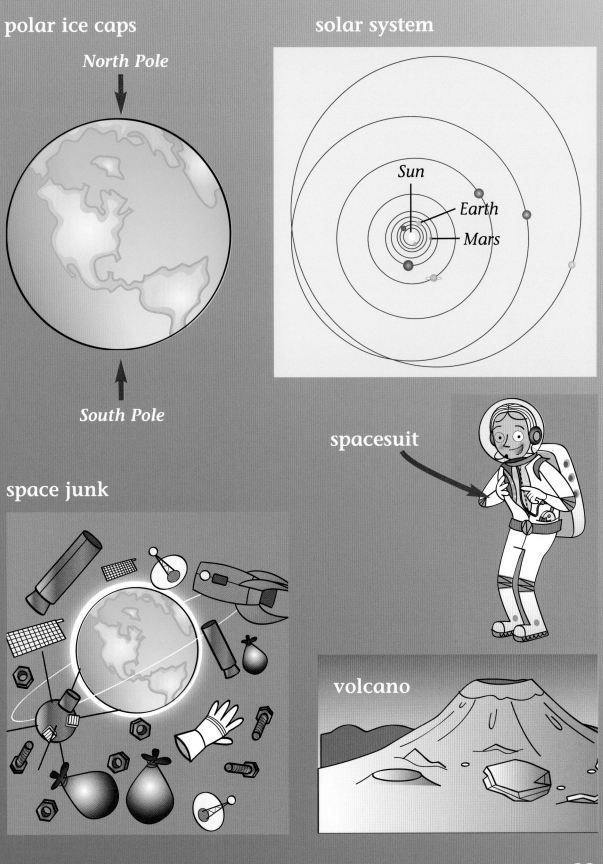

polar ice caps

North Pole

South Pole

solar system

Sun

Earth

Mars

spacesuit

space junk

volcano

✿ Ideas for reading ✿

Written by Linda Pagett B.Ed(hons), M.Ed
Lecturer and Educational Consultant

Learning objectives: generate questions before reading and use knowledge of books to retrieve information; understand fact/fiction; use a contents page to find way around text; use glossaries to locate words; use new words from reading linked to particular topics; present work from other parts of the curriculum for members of the class.

Curriculum links:
Numeracy: Shape, space and measure;

Science: forces and movement;
Geography: contrast with local area

Interest words:
amount, different, Martian, entertainment, designer, parachute, bargain

Word count: 782

Resources: whiteboards and pens, tape recorder

Getting started

This book may be read over two sessions.

- Ask the children if they've ever wanted to travel into space. Where would they go? Then show them the cover for *Let's Go to Mars* and discuss the blurb. What does it remind them of? (It is a holiday brochure about taking a holiday on Mars that might be possible in fifty years' time.)

- Scan and skim through the book with the children discussing the following questions: *Is it fact or fiction?* (It is a fictional holiday, but presents lots of facts about Mars.) *What new words can you find?*

- Write new 'space' words on a whiteboard, e.g. *solar system, planets, Saturn,* etc.

Reading and responding

- Ask the children to read independently and quietly, and choose a child in turn to read a short passage aloud. Remind the children to use the picture glossary to check unfamiliar words.

- Observe, prompt and praise each child for fluency, silent reading and self-correction, and prompt to use picture, word and context cues to solve challenging words.